Embracing Maine's Untamed Grace

by

Dan Huddleston

Finishing Line Press
Georgetown, Kentucky

Copyright © 2025 by Dan Huddleston
ISBN 979-8-89990-040-2 First Edition
All rights reserved under International and Pan-American Copyright Conventions. No part of this book may be reproduced in any manner whatsoever without written permission from the publisher, except in the case of brief quotations embodied in critical articles and reviews.

ACKNOWLEDGMENTS

I would like to thank my father-in-law, Mark Kaiser, who helped me edit the poetry through 14 editions.

Publisher: Leah Huete de Maines
Editor: Christen Kincaid
Cover Art: Dan Huddleston, photographer
Interior artwork and photos: Dan Huddleston
Author Photo: Dan Huddleston
Cover Design: Elizabeth Maines McCleavy

Order online: www.finishinglinepress.com
        also available on amazon.com

Author inquiries and mail orders:
Finishing Line Press
PO Box 1626
Georgetown, Kentucky 40324
USA

Contents

A Journey of Soul and Grace 8

Woods and Sea 10

The Allagash Wilderness 12

Summertime in Maine 14

The River Calls Me 16

The Loon 18

Fly Fishing the West Branch 20

Twin Ponds 22

The Spring Striper Run 24

I Dreamed of Autumn 26

Joan 28

Whispers of Love in Cape Elizabeth 30

Maine's Living Heritage 32

The Rhythm of Autumn 34

Babbs Covered Bridge 36

Sugarloaf 38

Roots Hold Tight 40

Tranquil Cliffs 42

Silent Giants 44

A Jewel Unseen 46

Glorious Aroostook 48

A Red Delicacy 50

Ode to Acadia's Splendor 52

The Legends of Maine's Lumberjacks 54

Downeast 56

The Greatest Mountain 58

Mill Brook 60

Maine's Songbird 62

Beneath the Salty Horizon 64

Discovering Rangeley 66

Beacons of Heritage 68

Dedicated to my lovely wife, Alisann
She's the gentle breeze that stirs my soul,
My rock, my love, she makes me whole.
The splendor of Maine, she helps me see,
But my only love, she'll forever be.

A JOURNEY OF SOUL AND GRACE

In Maine's embrace, a journey unfolds,
To rediscover a soul, once lost in the cold,
Its beauty beckons, an irresistible call,
To mend the spirit, to heal and enthrall.

Nature's hideaway, a balm for heartbreak,
Where whispers of wildlife tenderly partake,
In forests deep, solace is found,
As the soul finds solace, earthbound.

The rocky coast, with its rugged might,
Humbles the mind, casting shadows of light,
Teaching us our place in the grand scheme,
In the vastness of life, a humble dream.

The cold, powerful seas, they teach us anew,
The fragility of life, its cycles and hues,
With every crashing wave, a lesson is unveiled,
To cherish each moment, before it is veiled.

But in golden Summers, a balm for the soul,
Maine's embrace, her grace makes us whole,
It opens its arms to the wandering heart,
A sanctuary for wanderers to restart.

So come, dear traveler, to Maine's sacred land,
Let its beauty guide you, take you by the hand,
Rediscover your soul in its wild, untamed grace,
Let Maine's spirit ignite your innermost embrace.

WOODS AND SEA

Maine's character, defined by woods and sea,
In their bosom, its essence runs free.
Ancient woods whisper stories untold,
The mighty sea roars, a power to behold.
A bond unbreakable, nature's decree,
Maine's unique character, forever key.

"But always there have been the woods and the sea, and they have given Maine its unique character."
—Edward "Sandy" Ives

THE ALLAGASH WILDERNESS

In Maine's heart, where nature reigns supreme,
Lies a place of wonder, a wilderness dream.
Amidst the verdant forests and the sparkling streams,
The Allagash Wilderness Waterway gleams.

Here, the river meanders with gentle grace,
Carving its path through this pristine space.
A tapestry of beauty, vibrant and pure,
Where solitude and serenity endure.

The whispering pines stand tall and proud,
Their boughs reaching up to the heavens, endowed
With secrets of ages, whispered in the breeze,
A symphony of tranquility that puts the soul at ease.

The mirrored waters reflect the azure skies,
As loons sing their melodies, harmonies rise.
Dipping paddles glide through the glassy sheen,
A journey of discovery, a nature lover's dream.

The call of the wild echoes far and wide,
Through marshes and wetlands, where creatures hide.
Majestic moose graze upon the river's edge,
While bald eagles soar high on wings outstretched.

Campfires crackle, their warmth embracing the night,
Under a starlit canopy, painted with celestial light.
Tales are shared, laughter dances in the air,
As friendships grow stronger, bonded by nature's flair.

Through the seasons' cycles, the landscape transforms,
Spring blooms burst forth, vibrant colors regale.
Summer's embrace blankets the land with sun-kissed delight,
Autumn paints a masterpiece, a riot of hues so bright.

Winter's icy touch blankets the land in white,
A frozen ensemble, nature's hushed delight.
Icy footsteps crunch on snowy trails,
As the Allagash wilderness whispers its tales.

Oh, Allagash, your beauty knows no bounds,
A sanctuary where peace and harmony resound.
Forever etched within our hearts, your allure,
The Allagash Wilderness Waterway, an enchantm

SUMMERTIME IN MAINE

Amidst the tranquility of quaint New England,
Summer warms woods, a solace profound,
Wind whispers thru pines, a gentle breath,
An oft-missed serenity can be found.

In dappled sunlight kisses meandering streams,
Their melodies dance with the breeze's touch,
Fireflies weave their luminescent dreams,
In twilight's embrace, they shimmer so much.

Through emerald fields, adorned in wildflowers,
The landscape paints a masterpiece divine,
A blanket of hues, a vibrant bouquet,
Nature's opus, her beauty is mine.

The air, crisp and sweet, with saltwater's scent,
Caresses weary souls with gentle grace,
Each sunset, a canvas of radiant hues,
Touching the heart, a warm embrace.

From idyllic cottages to cobblestone streets,
New England's charm, an enchanting tale,
Where time stands still, and worries retreat,
A respite for wanderers, where memories prevail.

Oh, solace of New England, Summer's delight,
Where peace and tranquility find their home,
A sanctuary of dreams, ever serene,
In this cherished haven, our hearts shall roam.

THE RIVER CALLS ME

In the depths of my being, a yearning resides,
To leave it all behind, where tranquility abides.
A quaint river in New England calls to my core,
Its gentle whispers beckoning, forevermore.

My soul craves solace in nature's embrace,
To wander the banks, at a leisurely pace.
The ache within my gut, a burning desire,
To reside where serenity fuels my inner fire.

Words falter to capture the longing so true,
This wrenching absence, an ache I can't subdue.
The yearning runs deep, words fail to describe,
The pull of that river, where my dreams reside.

Oh, the bliss that awaits, in that tranquil place,
Where worries and burdens find sweetest erase.
With each passing day, the yearning grows strong,
To surrender it all, where my heart truly belongs.

In the depths of my soul, this dream takes flight,
To dwell by that river, where my spirit alights.
May destiny guide me, to that cherished scene,
Where my yearning finds solace, forever serene.

THE LOON

In Maine's secluded mountain ponds so still,
Where nature's tranquil whispers gently thrill,
There dwells a majestic beauty, proud and free,
The Loons, enchanting creatures by the sea.

With ebony plumes and eyes of crimson flame,
They dance upon the waters, never tame,
Their haunting calls pierce through the silent air,
A symphony of echoes, beyond compare.

Oh, how they glide with grace, like poetry in flight,
Their wings outstretched, a vision of pure delight,
Adorned with elegance, they paint the scene,
Reflecting the moon's glow, ethereal and serene.

Amidst the misty morn and golden rays,
They dive beneath the depths, where secrets sway,
Emerging with a silver fish, their prize,
A testament to nature's grandest guise.

The Loons, majestic symbols of the wild,
Their presence speaks of harmony, undefiled,
In Maine's secluded mountain ponds, they dwell,
A gift of nature's art, a story to tell.

So let us pause and cherish this grand sight,
The Loons, enchanting souls, a true delight,
For in their dance upon the water's sheen,
We find a glimpse of heaven, a tranquil dream.

FLY FISHING THE WEST BRANCH

Down the old Golden Road, Dad and I embark,
Autumn's whispers guide us, a journey marked.
Together, we drive with stories to unfold,
A bond of love and adventure, never to withhold.

The misty morning veils the West Branch's might,
As we cast our hopes upon its shimmering light.
Father's wisdom flows, a mentor by my side,
In pursuit of elusive trout, our spirits ride.

The sun unveils its warmth, fog gently departs,
Revealing nature's canvas, where beauty imparts.
Ripogenous Gorge beckons, a scenic retreat,
A sanctuary of colors, where souls find their beat.

Amidst the rushing waters, a symphony untamed,
We stand in awe, our hearts forever framed.
The fiery foliage surrounds us in vibrant embrace,
Nature's palette unfolds, a masterpiece's grace.

Father and child, united in awe-struck delight,
Nature's grandeur ignites our spirits, burning bright.
With each cast of the line, memories intertwine,
Along the Golden Road, a bond that's so divine.

Together we wander, nature's treasures we seek,
In this timeless bond, love's melody shall speak.

TWIN PONDS

In the realm of Maine, where nature holds its sway,
A sanctuary of peace, where tranquility holds sway,
Big Moose Pond and Little Moose Pond, nestled serene,
Their stillness whispers tales, of a tranquil scene.

Upon these secluded mountain ponds, pristine and clear,
Where crystal waters mirror heavens so near,
Primitive campgrounds invite the daring soul,
To embrace nature's wildness, untamed and whole.

A winding trail meanders steadfast and true,
Guiding explorers to vistas they pursue,
Atop the rock face, Earth unfolds her might,
Twin ponds and Big Moose Mountain, nature's precious light.

In the hush of mountains, where solitude prevails,
These ponds weave enchantment with nature's sacred tales,
As wanderers embark, glimpses of heavenly grace,
Big Moose Pond and Little Moose Pond, radiant in their embrace.

THE SPRING STRIPER RUN

Mid-May's surf, stripers come to town,
Higgins Beach, where anglers gather 'round,
In waters deep, where stripers roam,
A dance unfolds, a quest for home.

With patience and skill, the angler waits,
For the tide to right, flushing out bait,
Till finally, with a mighty splash,
Striped bass succumb to the angler's grasp.

In tales retold by fireside glow,
The story of the stripers caught will grow,
For in these waters where legends breed,
Anglers find solace, their spirits freed.

I DREAMED OF AUTUMN

In quiet old Maine, I dreamed of Autumn,
That fleeting respite, before Winter's doldrum.
The turning leaves, a painter's dream,
On back roads, the scenes I longed to gleam.

Autumn's wind, a touch upon my skin,
Piercing through my cozy sweater's thin.
The sun so golden, descending low,
I watched nature's colors begin to show.

From red to orange, to yellow's bright hue,
Leaves transformed, a breathtaking view.
The sun's rays danced upon each tree,
A sight that filled my heart with glee.

The crunch beneath my feet, a sound so sweet,
Autumn's wind, nature's ephemeral treat.
Raindrops fell, and leaves gently swayed,
As I trod damp trails, in the forest's serenade.

And then, as if in an enchanted trance,
Overnight, the leaves bid their last dance.
Bare trees stood, a stark and solemn sight,
Winter's chill replacing Autumn's light.

With a touch of sorrow, I bid farewell,
But cherished memories within me dwell.
The kinship forged with land and trees,
A bond I carry, as the seasons tease.

For in my heart, I hold the hope,
To witness Maine's Autumn kaleidoscope.
And when that time comes, I'll rejoice once more,
In the magnificence of Maine's fall I adore.

JOAN

In a small Maine town, Joan's heart found its beat,
Embracing the closeness, a community complete,
On dirt roads she wandered, a gentle pace in stride,
Small town life's heritage, where love and peace reside.

Neighbors were kin, sharing laughter and cheer,
In parochial haven, where bonds grew near,
Nature's dance enchanted, through seasons so fine,
Joan found solace in simplicity's divine.

Her roots were deep, firmly planted in place,
Small town allure, a cherished embrace,
For in this tranquil world, she knew her worth,
A testament to the beauty of humble birth.

In Joan's small town story, we find a truth,
In simplicity and love, eternal youth,
Her legacy a reminder, as time unfurls,
Of the power in the heritage of small town pearls.

WHISPERS OF LOVE
IN CAPE ELIZABETH

In the depths of Cape Elizabeth's chilling air,
The wind whispers secrets, beyond compare,
It rattles our souls, with its icy embrace,
Leaving us pondering, lost in its trace.

How do we live with its relentless blow,
Constant and cold, an unwavering flow?
We gather our strength, against its cruel might,
Seeking solace, in love's guiding light.

Moments elude us, even as we meditate,
For love's deadline hovers, an impending fate,
Her rocks hold still, their shapes intact,
While our hearts ache, love's course abstract.

But amidst this struggle, hope flickers within,
In melodies spun, a new chapter begins,
A song of resilience, of love's enduring power,
Guiding us through her tempest, hour by hour.

In the melodies spun, our hearts find release,
A symphony of longing, seeking inner peace,
For in the depths of the Cape's chilling air,
Love's essence warms, our hearts laid bare.

MAINE'S LIVING HERITAGE

The eastern white pine built the state of Maine,
A symbol of heritage and the land's untamed domain.
Tall and proud, it adorns the forest's green attire,
And carries the essence of Maine's history and desire.

In the days of old, its timber built ships of might,
Crafting vessels that sailed oceans, awe in every sight.
The white pine's strength, a testament profound,
To the resource that fueled Maine's growth all around.

From towering forests to the logging camps of yore,
The white pine stood tall, a beacon to adore.
Its needles whisper stories of a vibrant past,
Of lumberjacks and pioneers, whose memories will last.

But the white pine's significance goes beyond its wood,
For it symbolizes Maine's spirit, sturdy and good.
A reminder of the wild and untamed soul,
That thrives in the mountains and hills that roll.

The white pine stands as a guardian of the land,
A symbol of heritage, as only few understand.
Its very presence paints Maine's rich tapestry,
A testament to the state's identity and ancestry.

So cherish the eastern white pine, dear and grand,
Embrace its heritage, woven with Mainers' hands.
For in its branches lies a story profound,
Of this State's resilience, forever to be found.

THE RHYTHM OF AUTUMN

In the golden glow of Autumn's grace,
I stood by the river, a tranquil space.
Casting my fly, in the water's slow seam,
Lost in a world, time was but a dream.

The sun high above, painted the sky so blue,
And the water ran clear, revealing its true hue.
Trees adorned the banks, ablaze with fiery hues,
Nature's masterpiece, a spectacle to choose.

Amidst this beauty, a sight caught my eye,
A solitary leaf, on a rock nearby.
Submerged in the water, it clung with grace,
The leaf and the rock, in an intimate embrace.

In the depths it rested, reflecting the light,
A shimmering gem, a captivating sight.
As if calling out, to captivate my gaze,
A testament to beauty in its final days.

I waded closer, in awe and wonder,
Appreciating its journey, as I pondered.
From the Spring's awakening, through Summer's reign,
Providing shade and respite, nature's sweet refrain.

Then Autumn arrived, with its vibrant display,
The leaf's true colors on proud display.
Now detached from its host, it embraced its fate,
Drifting in the river, a dance so delicate.

Yet even in its journey, nearing life's end,
It inspired my soul, like a lifelong friend.
A reminder to cherish each fleeting breath,
And find beauty in every step until our own death.

So I stood in that moment, by the river's flow,
Grateful for the leaf, the beauty it bestowed.
For in its journey, it touched my heart anew,
A symbol of resilience, a reminder to pursue.

In the rhythm of the river, I found solace and peace,
As I witnessed nature's wonders, my soul released.
That solitary leaf, an emblem so grand,
A testament to love, in Autumn's gentle hand.

BABBS COVERED BRIDGE

In humble Maine, a majesty resides,
Babbs Covered Bridge, a cherished guide.
Spanning the Presumpscot with grace and might,
This wooden landmark, my delight.

Blue-green waters flow beneath its span,
Where trout run and spawn, a vibrant clan.
Children's laughter echoes through the air,
Swinging from ropes, with joyful flair.

I've cast my line in this serene abode,
Fishing for solace, as the river flowed.
A haven of quiet, nature's sweet refrain,
Where time stood still, and worries wane.

In Autumn's grasp, the trees ablaze,
A kaleidoscope of reds and golden rays.
The bridge, embraced by vibrant hues,
A testament to nature's chosen muse.

In Winter's shroud, the snow piled high,
A wonderland scene, beneath the sky.
Babbs Covered Bridge, in icy stillness,
A jewel in the midst of Winter's chillness.

Oh, the memories I've etched in this place,
Of tranquil moments and nature's embrace.
Babbs Covered Bridge, my cherished friend,
A symbol of heritage, as the river's bend.

SUGARLOAF

On Sugarloaf's slopes, I sought to glide,
A thrilling ride, friends by my side.
Crashes aplenty, at high speeds we flew,
Laughs and pain, a comical debut.

Through tumbles and spills, we found delight,
Falling gracefully, a comedic sight.
With each descent, my skills took flight,
From clumsy beginnings to skiing bright.

Patient guidance, their kindness true,
My friends, my teachers, helping me through.
They cheered as I mastered each turn,
From novices to conquerors, we'd adjourn.

Black diamonds awaited, a challenge untold,
Heart pounding, adrenaline took hold.
The thrill of speed, the rush of the ride,
On those icy slopes, my fears were defied.

Grateful am I for their selfless grace,
Guiding me to ski with skill and pace.
In memories we'll cherish, forever enshrined,
The day I conquered slopes, a triumph defined.

ROOTS HOLD TIGHT

The weather, not bad, for those who dare,
To endure the cold, a test of will and wear,
Photographs capture a distant Summer's glow,
While our grandfathers' true heritage echoes below.

In this place, motivation thrives,
To escape the stagnation, where hope's alive,
Dirt roads bear names of our old town's past,
While the cities' fast pace shows a contrast.

Time drifts languidly, but one avoids the stress,
Caring fades away, living on tranquil caress,
But when yearning grows, dreams await to believe,
Amidst what could have been, a heart finds reprieve.

In the house of upbringing, a final abode,
Homesick souls linger, their spirits erode,
The longing persists, searching for reasons to roam,
But roots hold tight, New England, a cherished home.

TRANQUIL CLIFFS

At Otter Cliff, where land and ocean meet,
Acadia's beauty, serene and complete.
The rugged cliffs, kissed by foamy spray,
A haven for nature, where memories sway.

Majestic and bold, the rocks stand tall,
Witnessing sunsets, casting a golden pall.
Seabirds glide, in the crisp ocean air,
Nature's symphony, a melody rare.

The crashing waves, with relentless might,
Carve the coastline, in their timeless fight.
Here, harmony thrives, in nature's grand art,
Otter Cliff's allure, etched in every heart.

So come, wanderer, to this sacred place,
Embrace the serenity, with every pace.
Acadia's gem, where dreams take flight,
Otter Cliff's embrace, a pure delight.

SILENT GIANTS

In the North Maine Woods, a majestic sight,
Where moose roam freely, in soft moonlight.
Their noble antlers, towering and grand,
Symbolizing strength, across the land.

Silent giants, amidst the forest's embrace,
Graceful and gentle, with quiet grace.
Their size commands respect, yet they remain,
Harbingers of peace, a tranquil domain.

Through meadows and streams, they wander free,
The contrabass of nature's symphony.
Their presence, a reminder, to cherish and protect,
The wilderness they call home, so perfect.

Oh, North Maine Woods, where moose reside,
A testament to nature's abundant pride.
May these majestic creatures forever embrace,
The land they roam, with their timeless grace

A JEWEL UNSEEN

In hidden streams, a treasure gleams,
Maine's native trout, vibrant beams.
With speckled coat, it gracefully glides,
A symbol of nature's untamed tides.

From icy waters, it swiftly weaves,
Master of stealth, where beauty breathes.
A legacy etched in timeless flow,
Maine's native trout, a jewel to know.

In mossy banks, its secrets lie,
A connection to wild, age-old and wise.
A symbol of resilience, pure and strong,
May its presence endure, forever belong.

Oh, Maine's native trout, unseen and rare,
A cherished gift beyond compare.
In depths so clear, its story unfolds,
A testament to nature's wonders untold.

GLORIOUS AROOSTOOK

On Maine's soil, a battle's call,
Soldiers rise, ready to stand tall.
Clouds of war loom in the air,
Invading frontiers, a solemn affair.

The soil, purchased by blood and toil,
Echoes the struggles, the settlers' foil.
Amidst the cries, does anyone hail
The British, who bring an unjust tale?

No, not these old landmarks, we declare,
For the scriptures guide us, a different share.
The sons of Columbia, west of the line,
United and strong, their cause aligns.

In Maine's defense, they take their stand,
Protecting the freedom, their sacred land.
The Aroostook War, a chapter's mark,
Courageous hearts shine, even in the dark.

A RED DELICACY

In Maine's waters, lobsters reside,
With beady eyes and claws spread wide.
Their pinch is fierce, but don't you fret,
For a delicious feast, they're worth the threat.

With butter and lemon, we prepare,
These crustaceans, beyond compare.
They scuttle around, in their underwater abode,
But when dinner's served, they hit the road.

From ocean depths to kitchen pots,
Lobsters face a steamy, buttery plot.
They wiggle their tails, as if to say,
"Enjoy us now, before we scuttle away!"

With bibs tied tight and crackers in hand,
We crack those shells, a lobster feast so grand.
Juicy meat bursts forth, a savory delight,
Messy fingers and happy faces, a joyful sight.

So raise your claws and give a cheer,
For Maine lobsters, oh so dear.
They bring laughter and flavor, in every bite,
A tasty adventure, day or night!

ODE TO ACADIA'S SPLENDOR

Oh, Acadia! Thy beauty knows no bound,
A gem of nature, where wonders abound.
Thy rugged cliffs, kissed by the ocean's breeze,
Enchant the soul, with each passing seize.

Majestic mountains, reaching for the sky,
Stand tall, as time and tides go by.
Thy forests dense, where echoes of the past,
Whisper tales of glory, destined to last.

In thy meadows green, wildflowers bloom,
A vibrant palette, dispelling all gloom.
With delicate grace, they sway in the wind,
A splendor of colors harmoniously pinned.

Oh, Acadia! Thy lakes and ponds serene,
Mirror the heavens, a tranquil scene.
As sunbeams dance upon thy mirrored face,
Reflections of grace and ethereal grace.

Thy trails meander through woods profound,
Leading adventurers, both lost and found.
With every step, a connection unfolds,
Between nature's wonders and mortal souls.

Oh, Acadia! Thy lighthouses stand,
Guiding ships home, with a steadfast hand.
Through stormy nights and foggy shroud,
They illuminate the way, proud and endowed.

Thy essence captured in each sunset's glow,
A masterpiece painted, for all to know.

THE LEGENDS OF MAINE'S LUMBERJACKS

In Maine's woodlands tall and grand,
Lumberjacks wield their mighty hand.
With strength they toil, their axes swung,
In deep forests, their songs are sung.

With arms of steel and souls unyielding,
Felling trees, their stories revealing.
With dawn's first light, they rise anew,
To harvest the forest, through and through.

Through rugged paths, they march apace,
Saws biting deep, timber to embrace.
In rain or snow, they brave the weather,
Bound by brotherhood, strong ties together.

"TIMBER!" echoes amidst towering pines,
Camaraderie forged in challenging times.
In wilderness, where nature's tune thrives,
Lumberjacks find solace in their lives.

When day is done, 'round fires they gather,
Sharing tales, faces warm with laughter.
To bold lumberjacks, a heartfelt toast,
Their strength and courage forever boast.

Guardians of timbered land they stand,
Honoring heritage built by their hand.
In the spirit of Malloch, their lore,
Maine's lumberjacks, forevermore.

DOWNEAST

Downeast Maine, where forest meets sea,
Spirit of strength, as stories weave free.
Fishing boats brave tempestuous skies,
Lighthouses guide with unwavering eyes.

Heritage flows through villages quaint,
Nature's tapestry, where tales acquaint.
Sunsets paint the horizon in vivid hue,
Mainers' spirit whispers, ever true.

THE GREATEST MOUNTAIN

Mount Katahdin, majestic and grand,
Rising tall in Maine's wondrous land.
With rugged peaks that touch the sky,
A sight which sends our spirits high.

Cloaked in wilderness, untamed and wild,
Where nature's beauty is reconciled.
Endless trails, adventures untold,
Whispering tales of legends of old.

From roaring streams to ancient trees,
Her ecosystem thrives and frees.
Silent sentry, standing strong,
Guardian of the wilderness, where dreams belong.

Oh, Katahdin, your presence revered,
In every season, your splendor appeared.
A font of inspiration and grace,
A sanctuary where souls find solace.

For those who seek, you offer respite,
An escape from the world's hurried plight.
Mount Katahdin, a sacred place,
A testament to nature's eternal embrace.

MILL BROOK

In Mill Brook's embrace, a dance unfolds,
As nature's spectacle, a tale to be told.
The alewife migration, a sight to behold,
A journey of resilience, a story of old.

From distant waters come an ancient call,
Through rivers and streams, they answer, one and all.
Against the current's force, they push with might,
Navigating obstacles, driven by instinct's light.

In silvery waves, they surge, a shimmering tide,
With effortless movement, as they gracefully glide.
Each step of their journey, a struggle they endure,
To reach their ancestral grounds, pure and secure.

From the bay to the lake, Mill Brook they traverse,
A lifeline of sustenance, where their destiny converges.
Amidst lush forests and mossy banks they tread,
Nature's compass a guide, their instincts finely bred.

The rhythm of their presence, a gift to behold,
Connecting past and present, memories unfold.
For in their sacred journey, a cycle revealed,
The balance of life, by nature's hand sealed.

The alewife migration, a timeless refrain,
The grace of nature, where harmony's domain.
In this small stream, their journey finds its worth,
An ode to perseverance, to nature's sacred birth.

MAINE'S SONGBIRD

In the forest's stillness it dwells,
The black-capped chickadee, its story tells,
A tiny bird with feathers black and white,
A delicate marvel of nature's delight.

With cheerful song, it greets the break of day,
Bringing joy and warmth along its way,
Its chirp, a song so sweet,
Filling the air, a melodious treat.

Amidst the branches, it flits and sings,
A spirited presence with agile wings,
Through seasons harsh, it bravely endures,
With resilience, its spirit assures.

In Winter's chill, it seeks its daily bread,
Flitting through snow, where others may dread,
With boundless energy, it never wanes,
Finding sustenance amid frozen plains.

Oh, black-capped chickadee, a charming friend,
In you, a lesson we apprehend,
That strength is not measured by size alone,
But by the spirit that's brightly shown.

So let us learn from this tiny bird's tale,
To face life's challenges without fail,
For in the woods, where nature bestows,
The black-capped chickadee forever grows.

BENEATH THE SALTY HORIZON

In dawn's embrace, a lobsterman sets sail,
On the rugged coast, where legends prevail,
With weathered hands, a bond to the sea,
The life of a lobsterman, wild and free.

At daybreak's light, the boat cuts through the mist,
Navigating waves, where adventure persists,
In search of bounty, in the depths below,
Where lobsters thrive, their patterns we know.

The traps are set, with seasoned expertise,
A dance with fate, upon the rolling seas,
A livelihood carved by sweat and toil,
The lobsterman's spirit, unbreakable and loyal.

Through wind and storm, they brave the unknown,
Facing nature's wrath, their courage shown,
With every haul, their fortitude displayed,
Their lives entwined, sea and soul never fade.

From dawn to dusk, their labor endures,
Through the changing tides, their passion pure,
For the ocean calls, with its siren's song,
And the lobsterman's heart forever belongs.

In solitude and salt, a life they embrace,
Weathering the elements, a noble chase,
For in the life of a lobsterman, resilience thrives,
A tale of courage, where true spirit survives.

DISCOVERING RANGELEY

Reflections shimmer upon tranquil waters,
Mirroring the sky and the surrounding quarters.
Whispering pines sway in the gentle breeze,
Their secrets shared with those who seek ease.

Fishermen cast their lines in hopes of a catch,
Trout and salmon, their tales they dispatch.
Hikers explore trails, nature's labyrinth unsealed,
With each step, a sense of wonder revealed.

In Winter's embrace, snow blankets the land,
A snowy paradise for adventurers to command.
Skiing, snowshoeing, and ice skating delight,
As the landscape transforms with Winter's might.

Rangeley Lakes, where serenity abounds,
A place of solace, where tranquility resounds.
Embrace its charm, let your spirit be free,
In the embrace of nature, find your sanctuary.

BEACONS OF HERITAGE

Oh, Maine, your rugged coast adorned,
With lights, some majestic some forlorn.
Symbols of splendor, heritage, and lore,
Safeguarding ships, shining forevermore.

From Portland Head to West Quoddy's might,
Bass Harbor, Pemaquid, shining so bright,
Owl's Head, Cape Neddick, and more,
Their presence, a treasure, the state adores.

In tranquil grace, majestic and upright,
Sentinels of the sea, a presence so bright.
Their beacons shine, piercing the night,
A comforting glow, a sailor's guiding light.

Each lighthouse, a story etched in stone,
Witness to triumphs, hardships, and unknown.
Through treacherous storms and fog's embrace,
Guiding vessels: Be wary o' this place!

Commerce once thrived, trade touched the shore,
The pulse of Maine's heritage, forevermore.
Fishermen set sail, their nets cast wide,
Lighthouses watched, commerce their guide.

Oh, Maine's lighthouses, guardians true,
Your splendor transcends the ocean's blue.
Preserved and cherished, in history's embrace,
Your essence resonates, enriching this place.

Commerce, heritage, and beauty divine,
In your presence, Maine's spirit will shine.
Ode to the lighthouses, noble and grand,
Forever guarding the state's coastal land.

Dan has a deep-seated passion for the natural world, a passion that found its voice in the serene landscapes of Maine. Though his time as a Maine resident was brief, it was transformative, igniting a lifelong journey into poetry that began as a private endeavor to express complex thoughts and emotions. Maine's rugged coastlines, lush forests, and tranquil solitude rekindled a childlike wonder in Dan, fostering a profound connection with the living earth. This experience not only shaped his poetry but also instilled a commitment to preserving the delicate beauty of our nation's natural heritage for future generations. This collection marks the public debut of Dan's lyrical reflections on the subtle, often overlooked beauty that Maine so generously unveiled.

www.ingramcontent.com/pod-product-compliance
Lightning Source LLC
Chambersburg PA
CBRC101458220426
43668CB00005B/45